I0012199

Windows Registry
Scripting

Unlock Developer Productivity

Table of Contents

Chapter 1. Introduction

Diving deep into the heart of your system parameters and configurations, our Special Report on "Windows Registry Scripting: Unlock Developer Productivity" presents you an opportunity to truly harness the power of your computer. This meticulously curated report walks you through the labyrinth of the Windows Registry, focusing on the utilization of scripting to enhance developer efficiency. Be prepared to crack open the intricacies of Windows Registry - but fear not! This is not about landing you in a sea of complex computer science jargon. Instead, we keep it straightforward, enabling you to understand, develop, and implement practical Registry scripts, irrespective of your familiarity or expertise with this subject. Enhance your understanding, transform your productivity, and most importantly, empower yourself with this significantly untapped facet of Windows development.

Chapter 2. Getting to Know Windows Registry

To dive into the world of Windows Registry scripting, it's crucial to first understand what the Windows Registry is. The Windows Registry is a fundamental part of Microsoft Windows operating systems, providing a space to store configurations and settings related to the operating system, hardware, software, and user profiles.

2.1. Understanding the Structure of the Windows Registry

The structure of the Windows Registry is hierarchical in nature, much like directories and folders. At the highest level, there are five "root keys" that can contain other keys (like folders), which can further have sub-keys, and so on. The five root keys are:

- HKEY_CLASSES_ROOT (HKCR)

- HKEY_CURRENT_USER (HKCU)

- HKEY_LOCAL_MACHINE (HKLM)

- HKEY_USERS (HKU)

- HKEY_CURRENT_CONFIG (HKCC)

Each of these keys serves a different purpose and stores different types of information. For instance, HKCU stores settings for the currently logged-in user, while HKLM contains information about the local machine, including hardware and software information.

2.2. Exploring Registry Keys and Values

Inside these keys, there are entries or "values". Each value stored in the registry keys has a name, type, and data. Common types of data include strings, binary data, and DWORD (32-bit) values.

Most often, these values are configured by the operating system during installation, but they can also be modified or created manually. The changes can enhance system performance, modify the user interface, and provide many other customization options.

2.3. Walking through the Registry Editor

It's important to note that making changes to the Windows Registry isn't usually done through a text editor or similar software. Instead, System Administrators and developers interact with the Windows Registry through a program called the Registry Editor, a GUI-based software that comes with every version of Windows.

To launch the Registry Editor, press the Windows key + R, type `regedit`, and press Enter. You can now navigate the hierarchical structure of keys we discussed earlier. Right-clicking allows you to modify existing entries or create new ones.

2.4. Importance of the Windows Registry

The Windows Registry is fundamental to the operation of the OS and the applications running on it. When a program is installed, it often comes with a `.reg` script that adds necessary entries to the registry. Other software might periodically check specific registry entries to confirm licensing or behave differently based on user preferences stored in the registry.

This makes knowledge of the Windows Registry and how it can be manipulated crucial to developers, System Administrators, and even power users.

2.5. Risks Associated with Modifying the Registry

While editing the registry can unlock greater control and customization of your system, modifying it without understanding the implications can cause significant issues. One misplaced keystroke could render software inoperative or even lead to the dreaded "blue screen of death".

It's important to exercise caution when modifying the registry and always create a backup before making changes. This can usually be done from the "File" menu of the Registry Editor. In addition, you should only modify the registry in line with the developer's instructions or when following a verified guide.

In the following chapters, we'll explore some practical examples of how to interact with the Windows Registry using scripts, but for now, you've gained foundational knowledge of what the Windows Registry is and how it works. This understanding forms the base upon which we can construct more complex concepts and skills.

Chapter 3. Navigating the Windows Registry Structure

The Windows Registry can be likened to a giant dictionary that stores all the configuration settings and options for Windows operating systems. It comprises a hierarchical database of keys, subkeys, and value pairs.

Starting with Windows 3.1, the Registry is the central repository of Microsoft Windows for storing settings that both the system and the applications use. It's not just a simple entity you can browse at your leisure – it's a full-fledged database with complex architecture, access rules, and protection mechanisms.

In this pursuit, let's initiate our journey into the depths of Windows Registry, primarily focusing on navigation.

3.1. Windows Registry Hierarchy

The Windows Registry is divided into five predefined keys, also referred to as roots or hives. These are:

1. HKEY_CURRENT_USER (HKCU)

2. HKEY_LOCAL_MACHINE (HKLM)

3. HKEY_CLASSES_ROOT (HKCR)

4. HKEY_CURRENT_CONFIG (HKCC)

5. HKEY_USERS (HKU)

Let's dig into the nuances of these keys alike.

HKEY_CURRENT_USER (HKCU): It's specific to the currently logged-in user and contains profile information. Although each user is represented by a unique SID (Security Identifier), HKCU points to the profile for the user currently logging in.

HKEY_LOCAL_MACHINE (HKLM): Unlike HKCU, this hive is not specific to the currently logged-in user and contains configuration information that controls the system's hardware, software, and security.

HKEY_CLASSES_ROOT (HKCR): This hive is an alias for a section in both HKCU and HKLM and it stores file type and file extension associations, along with user-interface-related settings.

HKEY_CURRENT_CONFIG (HKCC): This hive represents the hardware configuration of the system as it's currently booted.

HKEY_USERS (HKU): This hive contains information about all users who have logged into the system, including their individual profile settings.

3.2. Exploring Registry Keys

Each predefined key can have innumerable subkeys, and those can have further subkeys, leading to a tree-like structure. Furthermore, keys hold values, data fields with various types of data. To get a clear understanding, imagine a hierarchical file system where the folders are represented by keys, and the files by values.

Practically accessing the keys, subkeys and values would need us to dive into the in-built tool Windows ships with – the Registry Editor (or `regedit`). This GUI driven tool not only lets you navigate through the Registry hierarchy but also allows you to edit the values, given the user has necessary permissions.

Remember that modifying Registry keys and values in an incorrect way can destabilize or even crash your system, hence always ensure to exercise utmost caution while making changes.

3.3. Understanding Registry Data Types

Windows Registry uses a limited set of data types to store values. Enumerating some critical ones:

1. REG_BINARY – This data type stores information in a binary format

2. REG_DWORD – This data type represents data by a number that a program uses

3. REG_EXPAND_SZ – This data type is a variable-length data string

4. REG_MULTI_SZ – This data type is a multiple string

5. REG_SZ – This data type is a fixed-length data string

These data types help Windows, or the applications, interpret and process the information stored.

3.4. Beyond Manual Navigation

Windows Registry is by default accessed via regedit, which comes with an easy graphical interface, but falls short when it comes to bulk operations, automated changes, or when the requirement is to work on a headless system.

As a developer, one can automate Registry interaction process using scripting languages such as PowerShell or VBScript. Microsoft .NET also contains specific namespaces devoted to the Windows Registry, making languages like C# an option too.

For instance, in PowerShell:

```
$regKey = Get-ItemProperty -Path 'HKCU:\Control
Panel\Desktop\'
```

```
$wallpaperPath = $regKey."Wallpaper"
```

The above script fetches the path of the current Desktop background image.

While scripting makes interaction with Registry efficient, it's essential to note that correct permissions are necessary to read and (especially) write data. Always ensure to run such scripts with appropriate rights.

In this in-depth tour, you've familiarized yourself with the structure and fundamental ideas behind the Windows Registry. Armed with this knowledge, you're now poised to embark on the journey of scripting and automation, helping to supercharge your workflow and maximize productivity as a result. Further, remember to exercise caution and agility while navigating or manipulating the Windows Registry, because, in many ways, it is the very essence of the Operating System itself.

Chapter 4. Understanding Registry Data Types

Before we delve into the creation and management of Registry scripts, it's crucial that we embark on a journey to understand Registry Data types. The accuracy and effectiveness of your scripts ultimately depend on how well you comprehend these aspects.

The Windows Registry is a database that stores low-level settings for the operating system and for the applications that opt to use the Registry. For any key in the Windows Registry, the associated data is categorized by data types, or values, that include Binary, DWORD, QWORD, String, Multi-String, and Expandable String, among others.

4.1. Registry's Value Data Types

Let's start with the understanding of different Registry Value data types that assist in storing different kinds of information including binary data, numeric values, and text.

1. **Binary Value (REG_BINARY)**: This type stores data in a raw binary format. It is generally used by the Windows operating system and not widely used in scripting. The structure of binary datas can be different for each application.

2. **DWORD Value (REG_DWORD)**: DWORD stands for Double Word. These values store data as a number and are commonly used for boolean states – with 0 typically representing 'OFF' and non-zero (e.g., 1) representing 'ON'.

3. **QWORD Value (REG_QWORD)**: A QWORD value is a 64-bit numerical value, commonly used in 64-bit systems. It stores data as a number similar to the DWORD value.

4. **String Value (REG_SZ)**: This is a regular null-terminated string used to store text. It's the dominant data type for storing user-

related settings, paths of files and more.

5. **Multi-String Value (REG_MULTI_SZ)**: Multi-String Values are a particular set of character strings. Each string is null-terminated, and the last string is terminated with a second null. Multi-String Value is widely used for various purposes, including storing file paths.

6. **Expandable String Value (REG_EXPAND_SZ)**: An expandable string value is similar to a regular string value in that it stores text. However, the expandable string can contain an environment variable, and the value present is expanded whenever it is accessed.

4.2. Understanding Binary Values

The Binary Value (REG_BINARY) holds binary data, most often a sequence of bits unique to the software managing it and undecipherable otherwise. Many keys and flags that reside in the Windows Registry do not strictly fall under a numerical or string-like format, being instead marked by binary data.

To manipulate this type of data effectively, one must have concrete knowledge of the binary data's structure required by the application because the binary structure differs from one application or service to another. This data type's difficulty and critical usage contrast with its importance: many important system configurations reside in these REG_BINARY values.

4.3. Understanding DWORD and QWORD Values

DWORD and QWORD values store numerical data. While they might appear to be similar, the significant difference lies in their capacity. A DWORD value can store a 32-bit number ranging from 0 to

4,294,967,295 or a signed number ranging from -2,147,483,648 to 2,147,483,647. However, a QWORD value can store a 64-bit number, meaning it can carry substantially larger numbers because of its larger bit size.

It's also worth noting that DWORD values are common in all versions of Windows, whereas QWORD values are windows-64-bit specific. Therefore, when writing scripts, ensure you're using the appropriate data type for your target system.

4.4. Understanding String, Multi-String, and Expandable String Values

String Data Types represent a special type of information that varies from numerical (REG_DWORD) to binary (REG_BINARY) values.

1. A String Value (REG_SZ) is a data type that represents text-based entries and can hold any string containing any characters. Space is also permitted in string data. Something as simple as a file path or as convoluted as a command line string for program execution can be held in a String Value.

2. Multi-String Value (REG_MULTI_SZ): This data type is similar to the String Value (REG_SZ), but it contains multiple lines of strings, separated by NULL (0). Each entry is separated by a null and the last string is null-terminated. This complex data type typically holds multiple lines of text.

3. Expandable String Value (REG_EXPAND_SZ) gets its name because this value contains variables that will need expanding when called by a program. In other words, any value you add within %" and "%" would be expanded by the system to reflect the current state at execution time. A common usage is in the file paths which include an environment variable.

```
For example, %SystemRoot%\system32 means
C:\Windows\system32 in majority of systems.
```

Fully understanding Registry Data Types and their peculiarities is the linchpin for effectively interpreting and writing Registry scripts. As we now grasp the different types of Registry Data and their uses, we can start developing scripts that accurately and efficiently manipulate the Windows Registry. As we continue the journey into the depths of Windows Registry scripting, this knowledge will help add sophistication and elegance to your scripts, ultimately enhancing your productivity as a developer.

Chapter 5. Introduction to Scripting for Windows Registry

Before we delve into the details of scripting for the Windows registry, it's worthwhile understanding what constitutes the Windows Registry and the role it plays in the functioning of a Windows-based system. The Windows Registry serves as a centralized hierarchical database that the operating system uses to store crucial information required to configure the system for one or more users, applications, and hardware devices. The data stored in the registry varies from user profiles, installed applications and types of documents each can create, property sheet settings for folders and application icons, what hardware exists on the system, and the ports that are used.

5.1. Getting Started with Windows Registry

The registry may sound like a daunting place for the uninitiated, but it's merely a system-defined database wherein applications and system components store and retrieve configuration data. The data stored in the registry have both keys (resembling folders) and value entries (similar to files). Like a filesystem, keys can contain subkeys, which allows the creation of complex hierarchical data sets (akin to deeply nested folders and subfolders).

For any user or system application, the settings and configurations perceive the registry as a unified tree-like structure, with nodes branching off into subnodes. Registry Editor (Regedit), a Windows-provided utility, offers an interface for reviewing and modifying the registry database, making it appear like a hierarchical file system.

5.2. Delving into the Scripting Aspects

Now, let's shift focus to the scripting aspect. Scripts, in the context of the Windows Registry, are executable sequences of instructions written in a scripting language. They are designed to automate the management and administration of the registry, thereby boosting productivity by performing routine tasks faster and more accurately.

Administrative scripting can unlock new possibilities; imagine you have a task of making a particular registry change on all systems in your network. That's a potentially time-consuming job if done manually, but with administrative scripting, it can be done quickly and without error.

Scripts are text files with instructions that the computer follows. For our purposes, we will mainly discuss scripts written in the PowerShell language, which is native to Windows and provides powerful functionality to interact with the registry.

5.3. Why Windows PowerShell?

PowerShell has been the tool of choice for many developers and system administrators for automating tasks since its introduction in 2006. It's a task-based command-line shell and scripting language optimized for system administration.

PowerShell extends the robustness and versatility of shell scripting on other platforms to Windows. It can access COM and WMI, enabling administrative tasks on both local and remote Windows systems, plus WS-Management and CIM to manage remote Linux systems and network devices.

Importantly, PowerShell allows for interaction with the registry, providing an array of cmdlets (pronounced "command-lets") specifically for this purpose. This functionality adds to our motivation to use PowerShell for Windows Registry scripting.

5.4. Exploring Registry Scripting with PowerShell

PowerShell's design stands upon the concepts of cmdlets, scripts, functions, and variables. Despite cmdlets being native to PowerShell, these reusable components extend their usefulness to other hosts, making it easier for developers to control and automate repetitive tasks.

Among the various cmdlets offered for registry scripting, some notable ones are New-Item, Set-ItemProperty, Remove-Item, Get-ItemProperty, and Copy Item. These cmdlets offer functionality to create, modify, remove, fetch, and copy registry keys and values.

As an example, let's consider the simple action of creating a registry key. This can be accomplished via the New-Item cmdlet:

```
New-Item -Path "HKLM:\Software\TestKey"
```

In this command, "HKLM:\Software\TestKey" is the registry path where "HKLM" corresponds to HKEY_LOCAL_MACHINE, one of the root keys. The "TestKey" is the key being created.

5.5. Deeper into the Labyrinth - The Advanced Topics

While the basic cmdlets offer functionality for simple registry manipulations, PowerShell scripting can handle more advanced topics. It can call externally defined functions, interact with .NET libraries, control flow with loops, and handle error conditions.

We can extend our reach with PowerShell scripting, handling the entire lifecycle of registry keys, complex manipulations, tracking changes over time, and managing group policies.

To conclude, as we're set to plunge deeper into this realm of Windows Registry scripting, we encourage both the greenhorns and pros to brace themselves for the journey ahead. Armed with this fundamental knowledge, the path to mastering scripting that can automate and simplify registry manipulations seems not only achievable but also enjoyable. We start with the basics but gradually build up to more advanced concepts, aiding you in unlocking newer levels of productivity and efficiency in your development journey.

In the following chapters, we will take a deeper look at how we combine the basic and powerful cmdlets to solve complex tasks, set concepts about PowerShell scripts, and even learn how to handle frustration when things don't just line up!

Let this be your guiding beacon in the hitherto uncharted terrains of Windows Registry scripting. With time, patience, and practice, before you know it, you'll be fluent in this nuanced language of systems management. With that in mind, let's dive in.

Chapter 6. Creating and Deleting Registry Keys and Values

The Windows Registry is a hierarchical database storing low-level settings for the operating system and applications using the registry to achieve an optional level of interaction. Managing Registry Keys and Values enables developers to customize and optimize their systems according to their exact needs. Creating and deleting Registry Keys and Values entails careful steps, as any deviation could impact system functionality. Let's explore the process in detail.

6.1. Understanding Registry Keys and Values

Before discussing creation and deletion, a brief understanding of Registry Keys and Values is required. Registry Keys are like folders containing Values, which are akin to individual setting files. Registry Values have a name, type (such as REG_SZ or REG_DWORD), and data.

6.2. Creating a Registry Key Using Regedit

Registry Keys can be created manually through the Windows Registry Editor.

To do this:

1. Open the `Run` dialog (Win + R), type `regedit`, and press `Enter` to launch the Registry Editor.
2. Navigate the hierarchy, or the Key 'folders' to the correct location.

3. Right-click on your chosen location, select New -→ Key, and input the Key name.

The above process creates a new Registry Key at the chosen directory, ready to hold new Values.

6.3. Creating a Registry Key Using a Script

Visual Basic Scripting (VBScript) or PowerShell scripts can automate Registry Key creation. Below is a simple VBScript example:

```
'Set objects and define the Registry path
Dim WshShell, regKey
Set WshShell = CreateObject("WScript.Shell")
regKey = "HKEY_CURRENT_USER\Software\NewKey"

'Create the Registry Key
WshShell.RegWrite regKey & "\"
```

Save the above as a .vbs file and run it to create the NewKey under HKEY_CURRENT_USER\Software.

6.4. Creating a Registry Value

Creating a Registry Value follows the same patterns as creating Keys but includes defining a type and value. Using our previous VBScript example, a REG_SZ Value named TestValue containing the data This is a test can be added as shown:

```
'Set objects and define the Registry path
Dim WshShell, regKey
Set WshShell = CreateObject("WScript.Shell")
```

18

```
regKey = "HKEY_CURRENT_USER\Software\NewKey\TestValue"

'Create the Registry Key and Value
WshShell.RegWrite regKey, "This is a test", "REG_SZ"
```

The above script creates a TestValue Registry Value under NewKey.

6.5. Deleting Registry Keys and Values

Caution is necessary when deleting Registry Keys or Values since removal can impact system functionality.

This can be done manually:

1. Navigate to the Key or Value using regedit
2. Right click the Key or Value
3. Select Delete

Alternatively, VBScript or PowerShell scripts can automate the process. A simple VBScript to delete a Key:

```
'Set objects and define the Registry path
Dim WshShell, regKey
Set WshShell = CreateObject("WScript.Shell")
regKey = "HKEY_CURRENT_USER\Software\NewKey"

'Delete the Registry Key
WshShell.RegDelete regKey & "\"
```

This script deletes the NewKey Registry Key under HKEY_CURRENT_USER\Software. Similar methodology can delete a Value by pointing the script to the specific Value instead of the Key.

6.6. Summary

Managing Windows Registry can prove to be a powerful tool in the hands of developers, allowing customization and optimization of systems. However, the potential to hinder system performance necessitates caution and backup before implementing changes. With newfound understanding, creating and deleting Registry Keys and Values can empower developers, enhancing system efficiency.

Remember: the Windows Registry is potent and requires careful handling. Always back up your Registry before making changes. The power unlocked by understanding and managing the Registry offers boundless potential for system control and customization, representing a major stride toward mastering Windows development. Treat it with respect. Handle with care. Use it wisely.

Chapter 7. Modifying Registry Entries with Scripting

When working with scripting for the Windows Registry, one of the key operations you'll do is modifying registry values. Through the use of scripting, these changes can be automated, saving significant time and reducing the potential for human error.

7.1. Understanding Registry Entries

Before jumping into writing scripts, it's crucial to deepen one's understanding of registry entries. A registry entry consists of a key-value pair stored in the registry database, where a value can contain data of various types. Microsoft implements data types such as String, Binary, DWORD, QWORD, Multi-String, and Expandable String. The data you want to manipulate dictates the type of value you use.

7.2. PowerShell and the Windows Registry

PowerShell is a powerful tool for interacting with the Windows Registry. It offers cmdlets that allow you to navigate through the registry hierarchy, create, modify, and delete keys and values.

PowerShell's principal cmdlets for registry operation include `Get-Item`, `New-Item`, `Remove-Item`, `Set-Item`, `Get-ItemProperty`, `Set-ItemProperty`, `New-ItemProperty`, and `Remove-ItemProperty`.

7.3. Changing Value With `Set-ItemProperty`

The PowerShell cmdlet `Set-ItemProperty` principally handles the modification of registry values. Its syntax is relatively straightforward:

```
Set-ItemProperty -Path "Registry::FullPathToKey" -Name
"ValueName" -Value "NewValue"
```

The -Path parameter specifies the registry key you want to alter. -Name is the name of the value to modify, and -Value serves to define the new data to be set.

Let's modify a registry entry using the Set-ItemProperty. The registry key HKEY_CURRENT_USER\Control Panel\Mouse contains a value named DoubleClickSpeed, which defines the time interval for recognizing consecutive mouse clicks as a double click. To change this to 500 milliseconds, use the following command:

```
Set-ItemProperty -Path "HKCU:\Control Panel\Mouse" -Name
"DoubleClickSpeed" -Value 500
```

Here HKCU: is a PowerShell drive mapped to HKEY_CURRENT_USER.

7.4. Working with Binary and DWord Values

PowerShell also allows you to modify values containing Binary and DWORD data types. The process is similar to that of modifying String values, with a few additional considerations for data input.

When providing binary values in PowerShell, they need to be converted into a byte array. Use the .NET [byte[]] type accelerator for this purpose:

```
$binaryData = [byte[]](value1, value2, value3, ...,
valuen)
```

Once the byte array is created, it can be used to set a binary value:

```
Set-ItemProperty -Path "Registry::FullPathToKey" -Name
"BinaryValueName" -Value $binaryData
```

DWORD values, on the other hand, should be provided as decimal numbers (not hexadecimal). Therefore, set DWORD values as you would normally set a String, Integer, or Boolean value:

```
Set-ItemProperty -Path "Registry::FullPathToKey" -Name
"DWORDValueName" -Value DecimalValue
```

7.5. Deleting and Renaming Registry Values

In addition to modifying values, the Remove-ItemProperty and Rename-ItemProperty cmdlets allow you to delete and rename registry values, respectively. Here's how to do it:

```
Remove-ItemProperty -Path "Registry::FullPathToKey"
-Name "ValueName"
```

```
Rename-ItemProperty -Path "Registry::FullPathToKey"
-Name "OldName" -NewName "NewName"
```

7.6. Handling Errors and Troubleshooting

Windows Registry operations are sensitive, and errors while modifying the registry might cause erratic behavior or even lead to a system crash. To prevent such situations, PowerShell provides error handling mechanisms that can mitigate these potential issues.

For instance, the `Try Catch Finally` blocks in PowerShell are used for structured exception handling. You wrap the commands that might throw exceptions inside the `Try` block, and the `Catch` block then handles any occurred exceptions.

7.7. Conclusion

Scripting significantly enhances the ability to modify Windows Registry entries, both in terms of speed and accuracy. PowerShell proves to be one of the most potent scripting languages for this purpose, equipped with cmdlets that allow for direct and intuitive manipulation of registry keys and values. However, remember to tread carefully in this territory - a wrong move can do substantial damage to the operating system.

Chapter 8. Scripting Techniques for Troubleshooting Registry Errors

Creating an environment that is both efficient and effective often requires careful scripting. When utilizing Windows Registry, there is much potential to troubleshoot errors and enhance applications using scripting techniques. This exploration aims to enlighten you on the different ways scripts can be harnessed to improve your problem-solving efforts in Registry scenarios.

8.1. Introducing Troubleshooting Registry Errors with Scripts

Understanding how you can solve Windows Registry errors using scripts starts with understanding the Windows Registry in itself. The Windows Registry serves as a vast database storing low-level settings for the operating system and applications that opt to use it. Such settings may include kernel, device drivers, services, Security Accounts Manager, and user interface from Windows.

Scripts, particularly PowerShell scripts, will prove useful in diagnosing and rectifying errors within the registry. They can range from automatically fixing corrupted keys to setting user permissions to averting possible mishaps. Let's first discuss authenticating error messages.

8.2. Authenticating Registry Error Messages

Before you plunge into deciphering registry errors, it's crucial to verify that the error messages you're encountering are genuinely linked to the registry. Many error messages may seemingly imply a registry issue when they are, in fact, associated with other elements of your system.

A PowerShell script can be programmed to monitor event logs for registry-related errors. By confirming error authenticity, you can concentrate resources on genuine issues, preventing unnecessary time expenditure troubleshooting phantom problems. Remember to make a registry backup before proceeding.

8.3. Identifying and Mapping Registry Error Patterns

Often, registry errors follow a pattern or are associated with specific actions, applications, or conditions within your systems. For instance, errors can correlate with the launch of an application or an update to your system. Pinpointing these commonalities can be invaluable, and a well-honed script can tactfully accomplish this feat.

PowerShell scripts, for example, can comb through Windows Event Logs to observe patterns of errors cropping up. By recording the circumstances and timing surrounding these incidents, a script can map out an incidence pattern, facilitating troubleshooting by homing in on the repeat offenders.

8.4. Running a Thorough Registry Scan

The next step involves implementing a thorough scan of the Windows Registry. This process identifies the specifics of the errors at hand, ensuring that your script can perform precise troubleshooting.

Executing a scan can require careful scripting, especially when identifying keys or values that have changed or exhibit health issues. You can utilize script instructions to navigate the hierarchical structure of the registry, probing key paths and making note of any anomalies.

8.5. Deploying Automated Fixes for Identified Errors

Finally, after all the hard work tracking down those pesky registry issues, it's time to deploy your scripts for fixing the identified errors. This stage might involve repairing corrupted keys, modifying permissions, or even removing redundant values.

PowerShell allows developers to not only view but also modify registry key values. It makes it easier to employ the necessary changes to fix a variety of errors and helps developers automate these fixes.

8.6. Developing a Proactive Approach with Registry Scripts

According to the age-old adage, prevention is indeed better than cure. So, why not use scripts to prevent registry errors from occurring? This way, you're not just fixing issues but stopping them from emerging.

Proactive scripting might include regular healthy scans of the registry, managing permissions to halt unauthorized changes, or establishing an event log monitor to alert you immediately of potential issues.

8.7. Debugging Scripts for Enhanced Efficiency

While scripts can exceptionally augment your ability to troubleshoot and rectify registry errors, you might find yourself in a situation where the scripts are the problem. In such scenarios, debugging becomes a prerequisite.

Debugging your scripts demands a keen understanding of coding and scripting principles, but tools like the PowerShell Integrated Scripting Environment (ISE) can be useful allies in this endeavor. With ISE, you can step through your scripts line by line, identify loopholes, and isolate problematic code segments.

8.8. Wrapping It Up

Scripting Techniques for Troubleshooting Registry Errors is an engaging landscape, promising fascinating insights and skills bound to boost your productivity levels. By comprehending and employing these techniques, you can actively manage, maintain, and troubleshoot your Windows Registry thereby bringing out the best from your system.

Systematically applying these methods will hopefully make your Windows environment more reliable and refined. With practice, you can become proficient, transmuting scripting from a troubleshooting tool into a trusted ally in your development arsenal. Keep exploring, keep mastering, and you'll find that the Windows Registry holds no fears, but instead a plethora of opportunities. So gear it up and transform those dreaded registry symbols into stepping stones for new learning avenues.

Chapter 9. Securing the Windows Registry: Best Practices

Every interaction with your Windows computer, from opening programs to changing graphical settings, is mediated by the intricate structure of the Windows Registry. While immensely powerful, the registry is also sensitive and can be a target for malicious activities, making it imperative to secure it. Let's walk through some of the best practices for securing the Windows Registry.

9.1. Regularly Backup the Registry

One of the most straightforward ways to ensure the safety of your Windows Registry is to make a regular habit of backing it up. This can be executed through the Regedit tool included with Windows. To do this,

1. Open the Registry Editor by typing regedit in your Start menu and hitting Enter.

2. Select File > Export.

3. Choose the location to store your backup and provide a name for the backup file.

4. In the Export range section, select All, then click Save.

A backup is now created for your entire registry, enabling you to restore your registry to this specific point whenever required.

9.2. Restricting Registry Access

Secondly, to enforce security, restrict access to the Windows Registry by defining user permissions. This involves identifying those who require access and granting it accordingly, avoiding blanket access permissions. To enforce this:

1. Open `regedit` and navigate to the key you wish to set permissions for.

2. Right-click on the key, select `Permissions`.

3. Under `Group or user names`, select the user or group you want to set permissions for.

4. Under `Permissions for Users`, check the boxes for permissions you wish to grant.

This way, you can manage permissions effectively, reducing the risk associated with unnecessary access.

9.3. Disabling Write Access

An additional layer of security can be incorporated by blocking write access to high-risk areas of the registry. Implement this with the `gpedit.msc` tool:

1. Open the Group Policy Editor by typing `gpedit.msc` on the Start menu.

2. Go to `User Configuration > Administrative Templates > System`.

3. Double click on `Prevent access to registry editing tools` and set it to `Enabled`.

This prevents potential attackers from introducing dangerous changes.

9.4. Regular Auditing

Keeping track of activities in the registry can provide important clues to malicious activities. Enable auditing to receive notifications on chosen registry keys. This can be achieved by:

1. Right-clicking on the registry key you want audited and select `Permissions`.

2. Go to the `Advanced` tab and switch to the `Auditing` tab.

3. Click on `Add`, select `Principle`, type `Everyone`, and press `OK`.

4. Choose the `Full Control` option, apply these settings.

You will now receive notifications whenever the tracked keys are accessed or modified.

9.5. Leveraging Anti-malware Software

The use of protective software applications can ward off most types of registry-based malware attacks. Free or commercial versions of Anti-malware software can provide real-time registry protection by actively monitoring and blocking suspicious modifications.

As you turn your computer on each day, remember that securing the treasury of the Windows operating system is as crucial as the digital tasks you work on. With the adoption of these best practices, you have already taken a significant leap in securing your Windows Registry, reducing the likelihood of debilitating manipulations that could adversely impact your system.

Lastly, foster a sense of continuous learning and improvement. Stay updated with the latest news and tips about registry protection and Windows security. The realm of cyber threats is constantly evolving – and so should your defenses. With these measures, not only will you have a secure registry but also a more robust and reliable computing environment.

Chapter 10. Optimizing Developer Productivity with Registry Scripting

A crucial aspect of enhancing productivity in any development process is fine-tuning the underlying system to work in tandem with the developer's needs and methodologies. In the context of Windows, the Registry is a treasure trove of configurations and parameters that provides uncanny possibilities for optimization. This chapter aims to introduce, explain and exemplify the methods of incorporating Registry scripting to optimize developer productivity, thereby helping you harness the complete potential stored within your computer

10.1. Understanding the Windows Registry

To begin our journey, let's first delve into what the Windows Registry is. It's a database that stores low-level settings for the Microsoft Windows operating system and for applications that opt to use the Registry. This repository comprises keys and values; akin to arrays, where the key is the array name and the value represents the data saved under that name.

10.2. Anatomy of the Registry

Within the Registry, keys are logically organized into a hierarchical tree-like structure. There are five root keys, also termed as 'hives', containing settings and preferences for practically all aspects of your PC's operating environment. Each hive further contains subkeys, boasting their values and data. Understanding this structure is paramount to navigate the Registry and create potent scripts.

1. `HKEY_CLASSES_ROOT` - Associates file types with software, and stores most of the data for COM objects.

2. `HKEY_CURRENT_USER` - Settings for the active user profile.

3. `HKEY_LOCAL_MACHINE` - Settings for the hardware, software, and security data.

4. `HKEY_USERS` - Houses the user profiles on the computer.

5. `HKEY_CURRENT_CONFIG` - Settings for the hardware profile used by the computer at startup.

10.3. The Need for Registry Scripting

Given the profound implications the Registry holds over system configurations, why the specific emphasis on scripting? Well, the answer lies within the nature of a developer's work. It's dynamic, requiring frequent adjustments to system settings to match evolving project needs, which can be a time-consuming process if done manually. This is where scripting steps in, automating intricate tasks while allowing wider system control - a developer's dream tool, wouldn't you agree?

10.4. Tools for Registry Scripting

Several Windows-based tools provide means to script Registry edits. These include Regedit, PowerShell, VBScript, and the command line via `Reg.exe`. Since PowerShell is a robust, versatile, and widely accepted scripting language for Windows, our subsequent discussions will majorly focus on it.

10.5. Fundamentals of Registry Scripting with PowerShell

PowerShell offers several cmdlets to interact with the Registry, such as `Get-Item`, `Set-ItemProperty`, `New-Item`, and `Remove-Item`. Below is a brief overview of each.

1. `Get-Item` - Used to retrieve the configuration or settings of a key.

2. `Set-ItemProperty` - Modifies the data in a value of an existing key.

3. `New-Item` - Creates a new registry key or a value.

4. `Remove-Item` - Deletes a registry key or a value.

10.6. Real-world Scripting: Increasing System Performance

To provide a real-world context to the use of scripting in the Registry, we will outline scripts that boost system performance. They will revolve around the "Performance Options" dialog box (found within the 'System Properties'), which stores values in the Registry.

10.6.1. Disable Visual Effects

To enhance system performance, visual effects can be adjusted. The below script disables all visuals.

```
$path =
"HKCU:\Software\Microsoft\Windows\CurrentVersion\Explore
r\VisualEffects"
Set-ItemProperty -Path $path -Name VisualFXSetting
-Value 2
```

10.6.2. Disabling Indexing

Windows Indexing Service can slow down your PC. Here's how to disable it.

```
$path = "HKLM:\SOFTWARE\Microsoft\Windows Search"
Set-ItemProperty -Path $path -Name IsIndexing -Value 0
```

These are simple but effective ways to inject performance into your system via scripting.

10.7. Conclusion

While the simplicity of these lessons might have belied the complexity of the Registry, don't be mistaken. With numerous keys and a host of values, the Registry is a vast ocean. However, with the scripting elements discussed, harnessing this powerful tool to enhance productivity is an achievable endeavor. Just remember - with great power comes the need for responsibility. Be cautious when changing the Registry, as incorrect modifications can lead to system malfunctions.

Chapter 11. Real-World Applications: Case Studies of Effective Registry Scripting

Computers are such integral and versatile tools in modern life due largely to the capacity of their operating system, such as Windows, to manage hardware, software, and overall system operations. At the heart of this management function lies the Windows Registry, a database storing vast amounts of configuration data for the Windows operating system. By exploring the Windows Registry and utilizing scripting, developers have the potential to increase efficiency and productivity.

In this section, we will explore real-world applications of Registry scripting, considering various case studies that highlight its effectiveness.

11.1. Registry Backup and Restoration

Firstly, it's important to highlight Registry scripting's functionality related to backup and restoration. The significance of regularly backing up the Registry cannot be understated. By creating a script that automates this process, developers can significantly reduce the risk of catastrophic data loss.

Let's consider the scenario of a software house where the development team routinely makes deep alterations to their Windows Registries. Effectively backing up and restoring these Registries can be a time-consuming manual task. However, a Registry script providing automatic backup and restoration capabilities proves invaluable - setting a time, triggering the process, and storing the backup data on a secure, designated location. The developer's efficiency can then be channelled towards more productive tasks, thus optimizing the workflow.

11.2. Enhancing System Security via Registry Scripting

Windows Registry also contains a wealth of sensitive - often critical - information that can be a potential target for attackers. A smart use case of Registry scripting lies in protecting this valuable data.

A multinational company battled a recurring issue: silent malware infiltrating their systems, which attempted to establish non-granted registry keys. The security lead devised a brilliant preventive strategy using Registry scripting. By scheduling a script to monitor the Registry for any unauthorized or suspicious changes, they could effectively detect and neutralize these threats. The script acted as an early warning system, alerting the IT-Staff to any potential security breach and taking predefined measures when any unauthorized change was detected. This greatly enhanced the organization's security posture and reduced their vulnerability to such attacks.

11.3. Performance Tuning via Registry Edits

Among the myriad of parameters stored in the Windows Registry are several that directly impact system performance. Tweaking these parameters can substantially boost the system's speed, responsiveness, and reliability.

Consider the example of a graphic design studio, where the artists faced a slow system performance issue due to the extensive hardware requirements of their work. The use of Registry scripts proved game-changing in this context. The IT team implemented scripts that optimally modified the Windows Registry parameters - among them, those regulating the system cache, virtual memory, and user load time. The results were nothing short of extraordinary, with a significant improvement in the system's overall performance, substantially increased efficiency, and a happier team.

11.4. Simplifying Software Installation

Companies often need to mass-install software on multiple machines simultaneously. A well-designed Registry script can simplify this process, ensuring a seamless and rapid installation experience.

An instance of this emerged in an educational institution, which required a widespread deployment of a unique software solution on all campus computers. Conventionally, this would have involved countless hours of manual effort. Instead, the institution's IT team created a Registry script that made automated entries, configured necessary settings, and eliminated the manual installation needs. It not only made the process quicker and less error-prone, but also ensured uniformity in the installed versions and settings across all computers.

11.5. Optimizes System Reboot Sequence

Lastly, let's explore how Registry scripting can enhance system boot time by tweaking the sequence of services and applications run at startup.

The scenario here is a data center dealing with high-demand network services. Each time the systems rebooted during updates or planned maintenance, the boot sequence service, by default, caused significant delays. The developers identified the services critical to the optimal performance of their systems, and with the help of a registry script, modified the boot sequence. The result was reduced downtime during updates and increased overall service uptime - a significant productivity win.

In conclusion, the depth and breadth of Registry scripting applications are indeed extensive. By exploring and utilizing its capabilities, developers can increase their productivity, enhance workflows, and even address high-level issues like system security and performance. The case studies illustrated here are but a fraction of the potential that Registry scripting holds. As Windows systems continue to evolve, the potential uses and benefits of Registry scripting are indeed limitless. Happy scripting!

www.ingramcontent.com/pod-product-compliance
Lightning Source LLC
LaVergne TN
LVHW051627050326
832903LV00033B/4699